D1362145

Under the Shade of the Mulberry Tree

by Demi

PRENTICE-HALL, INC. ENGLEWOOD CLIFFS, NEW JERSEY

Printed in the United States of America •J

Prentice-Hall International, Inc., London
Prentice-Hall of Australia, Pty. Ltd., North Sydney
Prentice-Hall of Prentice-Hall of Canada, Ltd., Toronto
Prentice-Hall of India Private Ltd., New Delhi
Prentice-Hall of Japan, Inc., Tokyo
Prentice-Hall of Southeast Asia Pte. Ltd., Singapore
Whitehall Books Limited, Wellington, New Zealand

10 9 8 7 6 5 4 3 2 1

Library of Congress Cataloging in Publication Data

Demi.
Under the shade of the mulberry tree.

SUMMARY: Retells an old Chinese folk tale in which a greedy rich man is outwitted by a beggar to whom he sells the shade of his mulberry tree.
[1. Folklore—China] I. Title.
PZ8.1.H666Un [398.2] [E] 78-15733
ISBN 0-13-936476-5

FOR JOHNNY HITZ

Once, long ago, there was a rich man who lived in a house by the side of the road.

The house was shaded by a stately mulberry tree. Every day the rich man sat in the shade of the tree and went to sleep.

賀德美

One afternoon a poor man came and sat down under the tree. The rich man did not like this at all. "Get up, get up, get up," he shouted. "You can't stay here!"

"It is so pleasant here," began the poor man, but he was interrupted.

"This is my tree," shouted the rich man. "I own all of it: the trunk, the branches, the leaves and the shade. Everything!"

I cannot possibly buy all that," the poor man thought to himself. But I might be able to afford the shade, and that might be even better. "Will you sell me the shade?" he asked.

賀德美

The rich man was delighted that there was money to be made. "Why not?" he answered quickly, thinking the poor man was a fool. He beckoned to some people passing by to help them agree on a price. After sharp bargaining, the shade was sold.

賀德美
賀德美

Every day after that the poor man came to sit under the tree to rest. Wherever the shade happened to be, the poor man followed.

賀德美
賀德美
賀德美
賀德美
賀德美

Sometimes he rested with his bull.

賀德美
賀德美
賀德美
賀德美

Sometimes he reclined in the rich man's sitting room.

賀德美
賀德美
賀德美
賀德美
賀德美

And often he invited his friends and their mules to rest in the shade too.

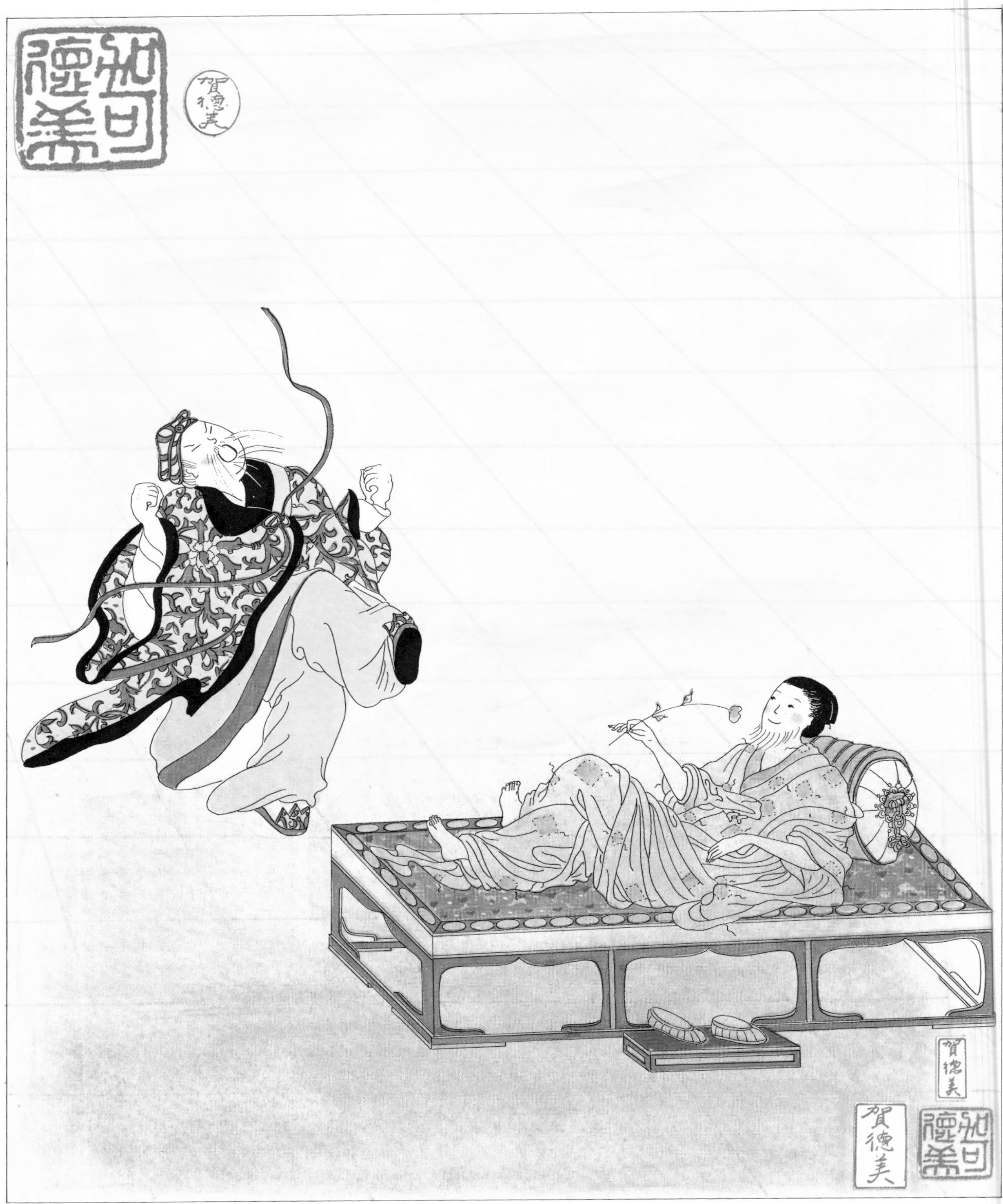
賀德美
賀德美
賀德美

A day came when the rich man could stand it no longer. "How dare you intrude like this into my courtyard, even into my house. Get out! Get out! Get out!" he screamed. But the poor man continued as before.

賀德美
賀德美
賀德美

One day the rich man sat at his table in the shade of the mulberry tree eating with guests. The poor man entered, with his water buffalo, and sat down at the table. When the guests learned he had bought the tree's shade, they laughed out loud.

賀德美

This was too much for the rich man to bear.

賀德美
賀德美

He moved away to another house where there was no shade.

The poor man moved into the rich man's house altogether, bringing his animals with him.

But he never turned away anyone who wished to sit and rest under the shade of the mulberry tree.

喜提士德美